Senses

of

Self

BECAUSE OUR MOOD IS FOREVER CHANGING

Author:Myra Shawnise Hollis
Illustrated by: Sarah Wright

Description

Senses of Self is a as needed, interactive journal designed to aid

you in both healing and reflection of the experiences you face

in life. Featuring various real life examples of letters, inspiring

quotes, and affirmations for support. This journal is the

ultimate tool to provide you support in your life!

This guided journal will help you:

- Process your current state of being

- Help you reflect on healing

- Heal from past issues that may revisit you

- Support your thoughts on your next move/idea

To use this journal you will want to identify a emotion/mood/

sense of self that you are experiencing. You will then focus on

writing to the emotion. The back of the book are prompts to

answer.

Dedication

Dedicated to my aunt Carolyn. Forever in my heart, thank you
for teaching me "If you want something you work hard until
you get it". My struggle in processing her loss has been
difficult but writing has helped and that is why
I am publishing my book now.

Foreword

Myra and I have been friends since we were in high school. We have seen each other go through many transitions in life. From being two young high schoolers getting our first weaves to young adults establishing nonprofits to adult professionals getting our master's degrees and traveling the world together.

I'm so proud of where Myra has come from and where she will go in the future. For the duration of the time I've known her, she has always wanted to be a therapist, so witnessing her get closer to accomplishing her dream while creating this book is incredibly empowering.

When therapy wasn't a realistic financial option, I depended on self-help books or books of essays on the human experience to help guide me through the situations I was dealing with. That's exactly what Myra has designed this book for. Reading this book will give you insight to what circumstances other people are in and how they manage with or without therapy. Not everyone is "normal", and nobody is perfect.

I remember a time when no one talked about mental illness. People would often use the term "crazy" to exaggerate or diminish someone's behavior because it didn't match their version of "normal". Today, I'm very thankful that talking about mental illness has become more mainstream, but there is still work to be done. Myra has worked hard to combine many stories together from people with a variety of mental health issues for readers to find at least one story they see themselves in. Be proud of yourself for picking up this book, you're one step closer to improving your mental well being. – Candace Armstrong

Introduction

As a marriage and family therapy student I learned how to tailor the way I do therapy with each of my clients to meet them where they are at. One thing has stayed the same across the board letter writing. When you think of letter writing it is usually to someone else. But do you ever write letters to yourself? If you said yes, great I would love to hear more about it. If you said no, this is going to be an interesting journey. Either way, you are in for some self-discovery, growth, self-compassion and overall a chance to envision and create the life you want.

Every day and every moment we are experiencing ourselves in different ways. Some more preferred than others. *"When we write things out, our left brain and right brain are able to work together to help us make better sense of how we feel."*

@haleyslone

In this book, you will read authentic stories along with letters that each person wrote in regards to their experiences.

TABLE OF CONTENTS

Words for those ready to embark on their journey:

"Therapy is to heal or treat and writing this Letter felt very therapeutic. Being able to process, understand, and see the growth of my feelings through reflection was and is necessary. I am hopeful that this book will be helpful for others to continue healing through others reflections and also self-reflect on

their own experiences."

Self

We are starting the book off with a simple

"Dear Self" letter.

These types of letters are powerful because any one at any age can write one. They are great to look back on and reflect. They help with reflecting the day of and even months or years letter. This " Dear Self " is more of a letter to create some calmness in the writer's day and affirming of the writer.

Dear Self,

Today has been a really rough day for me. There were multiple times when I questioned myself — questioned my worth. Times when I asked myself, "Am I good enough? Am I worthy?" In these pages I'll try my best to remember that through it all, I made it to the end of yet another day. The people, situations, and circumstances that make me feel unworthy are temporary — like seasons that come and go. I have to always tell myself from day to day — I am worthy! I am enough! I am resilient! I am strong! I am beautiful! I am loving! I am intuitive! I am rare! I am loved! Through these seasons, I am me and that's all I can be ♡

With love,
Self

Here is your space to write to your "Self":

_____

_____

_____

_____

_____

_____

_____

_____

_____

_____

_____

_____

_____

_____

_____

_____

Affirm:

There is strength in weakness.....

I AM ALLOWED TO FEEL

Anger

Have you ever felt yourself in a state of anger where when you look back you were surprised that you became so upset? We all have experienced anger in one way or another. But how do we tap into this anger and make sense of it?

Think about writing a letter to your angry self. Here is an example:

Dear Angry self,

We are here again with questions on is this my fault? Did I let my ang er get the best of me. WHAT IS HAPPENING. Other people struggle to understand what I am feeling and i often feel judged. But I have always struggled with letting things get to me, often teams I feel that maybe I am doing everything wrong and over thinking. Why don't people try to understand why I am angry? Are they not interested in my feelings? I know I just need to express myself, but the struggle is real.

I think back to childhood and the struggle to express myself and I get so mad that I still struggle but I know it cannot be all my fault . Sometimes I silence myself and anger brews inside. I feel hurt, broken and lost and DO NOT KNOW HOW ELSE TO EXPRESS IT. I tell myself to breathe but sometimes I want to scream. AHHHHH, LET IT OUT. I have to remind myself it is okay to be angry but it is also important to let it out and talk it out. LET IT OUT AND TALK IT OUT, I repeat over and over. Whew, I know it can't just be me. My anger will not get the best of me.

Here is your space to write to your "Self":

_____

_____

_____

_____

_____

_____

_____

_____

_____

_____

_____

_____

_____

_____

_____

_____

_____

Affirm:

It is ok to be angry

I WILL NOT LET MY SELF STAY IN THIS STATE.

Alone

Alone and lonely self may seem synonymous. You can decide which makes sense for you in your letter writing process. Here is an example:

Dear Alone Self,

When you finally are alone, meaning by yourself with no everyday interactions from others, it's going to be hard. It's going to eventually feel freeing but, first it's going to be really hard. This is what you wanted all the time when you felt committed to relationships that you felt overwhelmed with. Huhhhhh "I just want to be alone" … "I love to be by myself" you would say. Now it's here and it feels different. You live by yourself or have your own space. You pay your own bills, wash your own clothes, cook every meal, fix things around the house by yourself, clean by yourself, wash the car and take care of mechanical issues by yourself, ask yourself how your own day was, talk to yourself, drive by yourself, you go to work and when you come home you are.... yup you guessed it, by YOURSELF.

I am sorry you feel so lonely and your mind goes to such dark places. Of course you will die by yourself in your home and nobody will know for weeks because you are ALONE. Yes, you live over 2000 miles away from your hometown, where your family and ultimate roots reside. This will make it even harder to become adjusted to being alone. Writing this letter to myself I have come to understand the difference between LONELY and being ALONE. Lonely stands out as an emotion, feeling and state of mind that can change time and time again. Lonely is feeling like you are missing something, a piece of a puzzle. Lonely hurts and can make you want what you think others have. Another person to check-in with you daily, do things with, build with, grow with, challenge you, console you. Everyone feels lonely at one time or another. Now, alone is simply that, being by yourself.

You will learn that being alone is not a feeling for you, it will be behavior, motive, and I dare say it a stance. We live in a society where we are taught that being in a romantic relationship and having children is the end all be all in a socialization aspect. What you need to realize is that this is absolutely not true. You don't want to base your life only on what the society or other folks tell you it should be like; you have to figure out what that is for yourself. Life won't be exactly the same as others and this is your time to paint the canvas with the traits the Universe has blessed you with. It will be a rollercoaster and you many times will want to conform to society's standards of not being alone. But you will build positive friendships and be intentional about every relationship that enters your life, you will choose not to be around any type of person just because you are having a temporary lonely spell. Be grateful to be alone because you will understand your self so much more. You will hear and understand your thoughts and feelings ohh so clearly. And get the time to feel and understand your actions without having someone to sooth or agitate you more; of course, unless you choose to. Living by yourself will be a freedom that is empowering. You are ready for the World and because you have experienced being alone you know that it is full of bumps, twists, and turns, but you also know all the shortcuts to calmness, stop signs to process, and green lights to continue pushing through.

Here is your space to write to your "Self":

Insecure

We are living in a society where beauty standards are so far off from how we are identifying ourselves, in addition to dreamed of lifestyles. Our social media can easily play a role in how we think of ourselves, in addition to many other factors. We all have dealt with insecurities, and they may have come and gone or maybe even stayed. In the struggle of battling with insecurities, I ask you to do something difficult. Yes, write to those insecurities, place them outside of yourself and express how they are making you feel. Let it ALL out. Before you get started here is an example:

Dear Insecure Self,

You told me people were better than me. Told me I wasn't as smart, as likeable. You made me think I wasn't good enough and people I loved would one day realize you were right. You prompted and coached me, "Act like her, she's actually cool."

"Act like him; then he might like you." "You're not funny." "Don't be so goofy." "Don't talk so much, no one wants to hear your opinions." "You're not a star--don't shoot for the spotlight." "You can't, you don't, you're just not good enough." "They'll always find someone better, smarter, funnier."

You said if I wanted love, I would have to prove myself worthy. Said I had to convince them I could be what they liked. Said if they paid even the slightest attention that was enough. You said be happy with what I could get.

You steered me to people who knew you all too well, those who were complicit in your agendas. Insecurities, you made me comfortable with abuse. You said, "They're just insecure like you, have a little compassion." Said, "Remember, you're not even deserving, at least they'll tolerate you."

Insecurities, I can't mess with you anymore!

You nearly destroyed me. I almost lost my life because of you. You broke me down to nothing. I tried to ignore you and suppress your voice, until my mind and my body were full of your toxic energy.

I should hate you, for everything you tried to do to me. But now, all I really feel is shame for you. Because I understand you now. Your sole purpose is the ultimate destruction of the self.

You carry pain and darkness wherever you go. You stem from trauma--trauma that humans either suppress or ignore or are ignorant to. Instead of nurturing them, you mislead them.

You grew inside me from when I was a child. A child who was hurting and didn't know how to express it, who chose isolation, who lashed out through attitudes. A child whose parents didn't know how to nurture her hurt, who didn't know how to nurture their own because of you, Insecurities. I know the pain you've brought me, so I can imagine what you've done to them. I forgive them though, and in doing so, I forgive you as well.

I will no longer be a catalyst in your agenda to keep humanity insecure. I'm going to embrace you, heal every part of me you've tried to tear apart. I'm going to continue to forgive, love and inspire. Every day I heal, I learn to love myself unconditionally. I learn I am more than good enough. I am divine. I am truth. I am survival. I am knowledge. I am compassion. I am love and light. I am beyond worthy. I am a blessing.

Goodbye,

Here is your space to write to your "Self":

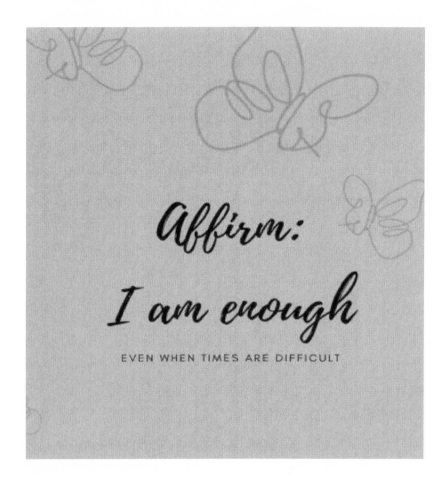

Affirm:

I am enough

EVEN WHEN TIMES ARE DIFFICULT

Content

It is a liberating feeling when we can feel content. Content is connected to peace and it can be a space of just being while not feeling a strong emotion of any sort. When we are content in life it is so important to write out those moments to go back and reflect. Here as an example of the writer reflecting on how they got to this space:

Dear Content Self,

So I was listening to a motivational speaker a few days ago and guess who it was? Yes, it was Eric Thomas! He has numerous videos but the one the caught my interest was the discussion about an alligator and how he can kill one with his bare hands. At first, I was confused but he later broke it down on how he can do such a task. Basically, once an alligator is fed, he or she is put in a coma. The alligator isn't hungry anymore and now it remains stationary with no fight, will or idea that while the alligator is asleep, the lion will continue to surpass this raging war. This is an example of my life as an incoming freshman in college to now a college graduate that has been out for two years.

For years, I was struggling with the fact that so many privileged players on the football had a chance to live out their dreams while I just watched from the stands. Playing football was always my dream so I knew if I continued to work hard, I'll be in the same boat as them. In my second semester of college, I tried out for the football team but I wasn't selected to become a part of their dynasty. I felt as though my time was wasted coming to this school so I started doing a bit bad in my classes. Unfortunately, I was put on academic probation and that really dimmed my lights. I was in a slightly dark place but I remembered the reason why I actually came to school in the first place. I was there to make my mother proud so I got up out that dark place and got off academic probation. I was relieved but my goals weren't completed just yet. I still wanted to play football so I tried out once again and got denied for a second time. After that, I was a bit over the fact that they didn't realize real talent and they didn't deserve a hard-working individual like me. After I left my try-out, one of the coaches gave me a pep-talk and told me to try-out again next semester because you did really well.

I told him I'll think about it but I wouldn't get my hopes up. I turned my main focus into get ting this college degree for my Mom so I put my dreams to the side for a bit.

When the next semester came, I contemplated on trying out for a third time but I could only look at the bright side of this situation. I have one coach that's cheering for me to make the team and I get a great workout for the day. It was a win-win situation for me so I went for it. Later that weekend, one of the coaches called me saying, "Congratulations, You were one of the few that were selected to be on the team. Show up for practice on Monday at 8a.m and be ready to work!" As soon as I got off the phone, my heart started beating faster and I couldn't stop smiling. I couldn't believe that my persistence and patience showed that day. I was grateful to the fullest extent and the only thing that was set on my mind to do was to call my family and friends because only they knew how much this meant to me. A few years went by and now I am a college graduate with two championship rings. I'm two years out of college and college football. The only thing I can honestly think of is football and getting back on that field. Being out of college and football for these past two years helped me reflect on everything I've obtained and everything I should be grateful for. It made me happy that I can still think of the times I struggled to get on that team. The battles I've had on and off the field. My support and love from my teammates, family and friends. The traveling me and my teammates went through to the different states of the country. The various kinds of food we ate before and after the games. I've learned that everything you plan never goes exactly as planned. It's a part of life but your reaction to every single situation you encounter will make or break you. My problems made me who I am today and that is exactly why I am content with myself. I couldn't be more excited to how everything went down because now, I feel as though I can make any one of my dreams become my reality. My willingness, consistency, persistence and prayers will get me through it all . with myself!

Here is your space to write to your "Self":

Motherhood

Motherhood is an interesting space to be in. Can one really describe? From my friends I have heard that it has rewards and also those moments of panic. Reflecting on this journey is something that can be passed on to those in our lives who may also be entering motherhood to remind them that the journey was/ is not easy and that you too have been there. In the letter this writer reflects on the beauty and hard parts; it is inspirational to see how to write even goes back to what she had hoped motherhood would look like. Check it out:

Hello there Momma,

I have to say, you really are trying your best to be a great mom. I know that at times you feel overwhelmed, but you always manage to figure it out. The greatest part of all is that your little girl is always watching and learning. You've made her feel important and loved. Years from now on, she'll hardly remember the tantrums and meltdowns, but what she will remember is how you made her feel, how loved she was, and how connected she was to you.

You always talked about wanting to be the best example for your kids, and here you are, making your dream come true you're raising a little girl who is just as determined, caring, and amazing as you. So don't be too hard on yourself. Slow down and enjoy these moments who cares if your house is always a mess Take the time to appreciate being a mom.   ♡/you!

Here is your space to write to your "Self":

Finding Self

We have all been in that space where we question who we ae and what we are doing and even if what we are doing is right. In these moments writing things out can help us figure out what we are doing and even vent that we are lost. The letter to the self who is finding themselves is important because when you are finally where you want to be and you look back and read this letter you will be able to say WOW look where I am now. Here as an example of this type of letter:

To myself who's finding myself:

It's okay you can't get it together. Can't get it right. Don't know why, I don't either ha. One day it will click for you. It will just all make sense. One day you will get tired of the bullshit and let it all go. But for now, sit in it. Every emotion, feel it, so that you will know how you never want to feel again. Those moments you make time to visit me are the best! Do you remember what it's like to be free? To smile because you're happy to be with me in the cool, calm quiet of the hussle and bussle of the world? Seeing the things you never notice when you're apart from me, like just how vivid the colors of the wind are.

A little bit about us. Our spirit is quiet and pure. Our vibration strong and overpowering. Sit in the quiet of the sunlight and close your eyes. Do you feel something different? Something peacefully strange? That's me. That's you. Keep track of all the new thoughts you feel in those moments of strangeness. It's not emotion to be dismissed. It's emotion that will drive you to action so you can get to me.

What am I saying? Stop doing things that don't serve you; you sell your soul. This doesn't give you an out to be selfish. You can still give while staying in your lane. When it's right; it will add to you.

Remember your values and then become them. It will be hard, but you are highly intelligent. I know you'll find me.

Don't rush, search safely and at a good pace. When you get here we have someone else to see.

To my future self: I hope you are everything we dreamed you would be and more. We can't wait to see you.

Love always.

Here is your space to write to your "Self":

Fearful Self

While some of the sense of self we experience can be easier to write about, some can be the opposite. Fear can be experienced for tons of different reasons and while writing about it may seem scary and can also be therapeutic. How you are experiencing fear in your life, I challenge you to write about. Write out every detail that is coming to you and give yourself the chance to experience every additional emotion followed by the fear. This writer wrote about a specific fear that she was facing and did not hold back. Check it out here:

Dear Fear,

Cold sweats- hot sweats- shivers- shakes- hair follicles constrict-heart palpitations… I gasped while trying to fight the physical manifestations of fear in my body. Feeling fear made me feel cut open wide and exposed. Being vulnerable and weak in front of others made me feel inferior. I thought about the long line of Black women that I come from. Did my mother feel this feeling when she had an emergency C-section because the umbilical cord was wrapped around my neck? Did my grandmother feel this type of fear when she birthed 11 children naturally? I thought about my great- grandmother and her mother before her and felt like the epitome of a coward. Strong Black Woman do not shake and shiver. I called my mother and she recited the Lord's Prayer with me. I confessed my sins to her while simultaneously being prepped for an emergency surgery. My mother asked me if I was pregnant. To which I replied, "yes."

I was an 18 year old unwed pregnant girl being prepared for a major surgery. I would not leave the hospital as an 18 year old unwed mother. I would leave the hospital with an eight inch scar painfully carved into my bikini zone, one less fallopian tube, and no baby. At 18 I had never had a broken bone. I had never been cut. The fear of surgery wasn't the fear that made me shake and shiver. I was split between the fear of death and the fear of shame.

My mother gave me unconditional love but so many other people had invested in me. How would they feel when they found out that I let them down? How would they react when they discovered that I was not the good girl that they thought that I was?

The fear of being shamed and rejected seemed to hit harder than the fear of possible death. My boyfriend at the time tried to com fort me by saying that, "everything happening for a reason." He said that the pain in my pelvic area was a blessing in disguise. He equated the jabs that felt like a strong forceful stiletto clad foot kicking me repeatedly from the inside to "God's will." He called the blood that I lost from my ruptured fallopian tube a "divine intervention." While he felt relief I felt more fear. This time it was fear about God. Was God punishing me for breaking his com mands? Was I afflicted with an ectopic pregnancy because of my sin? I completed all of the wrongs that I had done from as long as I could remember. While being anesthetized I wondered if I didn't make it through the procedure would I at least be able to make it into heaven.

A shot of pain woke me out of an anesthesia induced coma. I have heard that people who make it through some of the most fearful moments

in their lives become immune to fear. Here I was on the other side of one of the most frightening experiences of my novel adult life consumed with even more fear. I fearfully thanked God for sparing my life. I fearfully asked God to forgive me for my sins. I was frightened that my family would never forgive me and petrified that I would never know the joys of wifedom and motherhood. I eventually recovered and left the hospital 10 days later but I was never the same after that day.

I did not die a physical death. My self-worth and my courage died through that experience. My fears lingered. I stayed away from the people that loved me most and gravitated towards people, places, and things that sought to destroy me. I feared God's punishment. I feared failing again. I left the hospital physically alive but a little more dead inside. Of course I accomplished things but I always held my breath a little waiting for curses and tragedy to strike. I always envisioned the worst possible disasters happening at times when I was supposed to be celebrating and enjoying life. Quite often I experienced all of the negativity that I imagined and more in real life. It would take over a decade for me to come to the realization that thoughts have power. I had to learn to kill my fears as soon as they sprouted.

A battle ensued in my head every day. I had to learn to answer thoughts like "God scarred your womb because you fornicated" with thoughts like "I am God's Girl; he loves me;

he forgives me, and he has plans for me to be a mother to many generations." Eventually, God became my salvation and not a vengeful deity the sought to curse me. The people that I thought would reject and shame me were the same people that would come to embrace and encourage me to step further and further away from fear. I am still fighting fear and anxiety. However, I am now aware that I need a little help from my therapist and my community to quell the thoughts that once relegated me to the annals of unhappiness.

Fear is a natural human sense that helps us stay out of danger. Unchecked, fear becomes a self-constructed prison that plants deep seeds and sprouts like strongly rooted weeds. You have to fight to make the choice to reach past what scares you the most in order to get exactly what you need to grow. Dig down deep and reach past your fears.

Here is your space to write to your "Self":

Disappointed

I've been there and I am sure you have been there, the space in your life where you felt that you had reached all these accolades and yet still feel like you are not doing enough or are not doing the "right thing" whatever that thing is.

With that comes disappointment and disappointment is something that I'm almost positive is not new for you; what do you do with disappointment?   Try to make sense of it? Understand it? In writing a letter about your disappointed self, go ahead and get right into the root of where it is coming from?

I encourage you to highlight the key points that you hit and think about how you can change this narrative for yourself. Here is an example:

~~Draft~~ Disappointed   May 23, 2019

il have two degrees, a beautiful boyfriend, a few solid friends & I get the opportunity to travel abroad frequently. So why am I so dissatisfied & disappointed in in myself & w/ my life? Why am I letting my negative emotions take control of my attitude & relationships?

After recently graduating w/ a M.A.T. from USC, I moved to Israel w/ my boyfriend, who plays professional basketball. Over the course of the 6 months I was there il became more regretful, and sad over my past mistakes (which some view as "success"). I no longer wanted to be a teacher, I was so upset w/ myself for getting my masters in something so... simple. I wish I would have pushed myself more & went for something more promising and something I can be more proud of. This new found self-pity & disappointment has changed my entire personality Im less happy, Im less ambitious, I cry more often, & my soul has become dull Ive been trying my hardest

to get myself out of this funk. With the
encouragement & unconditional love from my
boyfriend I was able to start "wanting" to do
more to get my life back on track. Its hard
for me to see how my new spirit ~~has changed~~
has changed me. I'm not the same as I ~~was~~
once was & I'm terrified that it'll drive my
boyfriend away - I'm disappointed in myself
for not doing better, choosing better, and being
better.

Here is your space to write to your "Self":

Experiencing Change

Think about how you experience change, change can be seen as good for some and scary for others. We never know what is to come with change and that is okay. It is important for us to express our feelings around change so that we can process our feelings around it. Check out a letter below focused on change:

Dear Self, That is Experiencing Change,

Going through changes...which is something that you fear.

For the first time in your life, you have been forced to feel. Sit in your shit and wade in it so far beyond what you could have even imagined. It's been hard because God built you for survival. You have been taught to mask your emotions. You feel physical restraint when it comes time to ask for help because help is not something that is always available to you. The only thing that you know is pouring into everyone's cup from your empty pitcher, especially when you are dying from dehydration yourself. But that has slowly begun to change...

Your environment is now new and filled with people who foster a culture of care and put you and you humanity first. They see you for who you are and genuinely ask about your needs and wants. They understand the value and need of mental days, and understand that life does happen. You have begun to open up and learn more about yourself because you have gone to therapy. All those thoughts in your mind, that are amplified to you and muted to the world now have a safe space to manifest. The weight has slowly begun to lift. Those tears that you thought you could never cry are now invited and don't have a need for explanation. You let them flow continuously and that God for the ability to shed and lean into your emotions. Your sensitivity is on display, and it is powerful. You no longer see it as a weakness and allow yourself to truly be who you are. You are starting to feel. For so long you have been disconnected from yourself. Now that things come up, you are starting to understand and name what you are feeling while it is happening.

So although you have feared change all of your life. You are starting to realize the beauty of it all and sometimes that means sitting in the pain and working through it. And it's okay not to do it alone, it's okay to ask for help. It's okay not to be okay sometimes, but as long as you are being true to yourself and have a healthy environment and support system, the change won't be so hard.

I love you and pray for you everyday.

Here is your space to write to your "Self":

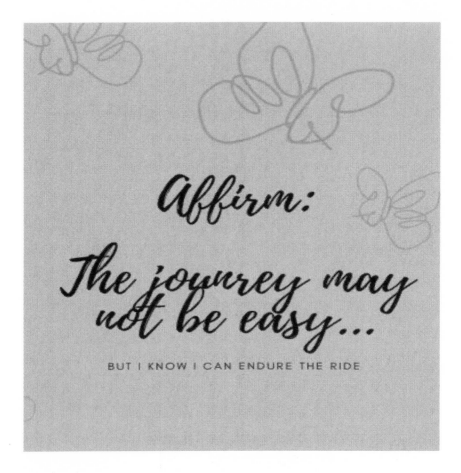

Affirm:

The journey may
not be easy...

BUT I KNOW I CAN ENDURE THE RIDE

Comfort Zone

Think what does it mean to be stuck in your comfort zone.
Does it feel that you need to push yourself to go further or does
this space feel good to be in? Sometimes are comfort zone can
hold us back and that is exactly what this writer addresses in his
letter, check it out:

Dear Comfort Zone,

What does comfort Zone mean to you?

Where does the comfort zone reside? and most importantly
why is it so hard to get out?! Some may call it a handicap, but
Others may call it a happy place. to each its own right? This
letter is to everyone hiding behind that gray jacket AKA your
comfort zone, which may be defined as a place or situation
where one feels safe and at ease and without stress.

With all this being said my comfort zone was my gray
jacket injury at Birth, called Brachial plexus Injury forced me to
move and think differently towards the things that God put in

front of me. with having this injury in my left arm it has caused me to Improvise and be comfortable with the uncomfortable. but why was it so hard to accept yourself and be comfortable around everybody you meet? Why are you hiding your arm? What is wrong with your arm? In the sixth grade after moving to Arlington Texas was one of the hardest times of my life. I wear a gray jacket everyday EVEN IN 100 degree WEATHER.

I was asking for a heat stroke . But just being around people who treated me as their equal changed the game for me. My mom and sister always reminded me that God made me this way because I meant to change your bra and be an inspiration to this world. but it starts with believing in myself. So I took off that gray jacket and began to spread my wings slowly but surely. I'm still dealing with this today but Rome wasn't built in a day and neither was I. If you're scared to do something, DO IT... I promise it's worth it in the end! Thank you grey jacker you tell me what it means to get out of my comfort zone.

Here is your space to write to your "Self":

_____

_____

_____

_____

_____

_____

_____

_____

_____

_____

_____

_____

_____

_____

Depressed Self

I wanted to make sure that we include a space to write to our depressed self intentionally because it is not who you are but rather something that you are experiencing. Depression is TOUGH, I will say that and also want to make sure that we have a space to remind you that you are not alone. Here is a letter of someone talking through their experience:

Dear Depressed Self,

Times are tough and so are people. You can try and be happy but we know that you arent or can't believe it. I know you are tired and sad but things always gets better. I know that somedays are worth staying in your room, on your bed sleeping the day away but that isnt living. I know that being outside is better even if its cold. I know that times can be stressful or even feeling blue but knowing that you can get away to the spot is better than staying at home. You can punish read, and not there just go there. When there are days you don't want to go to school dont go because its worth getting your work done then being behind. When you don't feel like going out and staying in bed at least do not go to sleep to waste the day because you wont feel any better but worse. I know that things could be better but if you think about it, it could be worse. You just need a little motivation to get up and get ready for the day, maybe when your feeling down go to the spot and breathe. I feel like that when I become my sad self I cant express how I feel so I think that if I keep myself busy and out of my sad mindset, I can become a little bit happier. I feel like I just need to breathe sometimes sometimes

49

Here is your space to write to your "Self":

Affirm:

I can find home
within myself

NO ONE ELSE HOLDS THE KEY TO MY HAPPINESS.

Hiding Self

Hiding self is a feeling that is not often thought of, think of hiding self just as it sounds holding back pieces of yourself this can happen in so many different realms of life. Take a second and read about how this writer experiencing their hiding self:

Dear Hiding Self,

I see you, hiding from the world because
you got too messy, and were afraid that
you were too much. Maybe someone even
told you that. I see you, hiding away
trying to get yourself right and feeling
like a complete failure.
I get that you feel unworthy and ashamed.
I know about all those little things you
forgot to do, all those things you wish
you hadn't said or done. And guess
what? I love you exactly as you are.
I understand. But you have to let
yourself ugly cry and forgive yourself
for not meeting your own too-high
expectations. You are the only one
who can heal you, you are
not broken. Actually, you are
radiant in all your messy
imperfections. Breathe.
Let yourself be vulnerable, and let
your trusted loved ones see you like
this. Show yourself as much kindness
as you show others; you have the
courage to be seen. And in case you
didn't know, you are loved exactly
as you are.

Here is your space to write to your "Self":

Pick Me Up

You are the author of your life and know what you need. Take some time to write to yourself to give yourself some words on what you need. Here is an example of a letter to write to yourself:

Dear Self Who Needs A Little Pick Me Up,

Good morning! Remember that this is a day the Lord has made. Rejoice in knowing that you are loved by God, by your family, by your friends.

Do not let doubt, fear, and insecurities inhibit your growth to day and tomorrow. Take anything that comes as a lesson and re member you are learning. You are a beautifully flawed human... REMEMBER YOU ARE A HUMAN. You're not perfect and no one demands or expects perfection of you. Stop and do not de mand perfection of yourself, but instead demand greatness and valiant efforts.

Remember to show and give yourself compassion,

understanding, and empathy. Forgive yourself, as you forgive your peers. Love yourself because you are great. You are great because God made you. Live out this day remembering to exhibit and be fruitful in spirit. Remember not only to be fruitful in speech, but also in thought and action. For who you think you are, you shall become.

I'm here to remind you that no matter where you are emotionally today, you are a wonderful person. You are a kind, caring and giving person. You are tender hearted and loving. You have flaws as anyone does, but I want you to focus on the things that you do well and the qualities that are great-you've spent too much of your life thinking of yourself in the context of your faults and your flaws, which can stunt your growth and journey of self love Seek validation from God above any and all else - the rest will follow suit.

Hey you! - you can win! You will overcome! Weapons may form, but God promised they would not prosper. Rebuke all negativity and shield yourself in the knowledge of His word and His love for you.

Here is your space to write to your "Self":

Boundary Setting

How do we know when to set boundaries? Boundary setting is often times not taught to us we kind of just learn it. Or at least I had to just learn it and have heard the same from others. Boundary setting can be liberating and also a form of selfcare

Dear Boundary Setting Self,

Within the last two years, I found myself reflecting a lot on the notion of setting boundaries. What are the discourses that come to mind when thinking about setting boundaries? What connotations do actions around setting boundaries have? What does set ting boundaries look like? How does it impact us personally and relationally?

In an attempt to negotiate the term "boundaries" in a way that is more fitting for me, a way that represents what I would call what I am doing when I am "setting boundaries", I came to know that an experience-near definition of "boundaries" for me would be calling it "preferences". If we looked at boundaries as pathways that guide us towards our preferences and towards our preferred ways of relating to others and the world around us, maybe even a preferred way of relating to ourselves, I imagine that our relationship to this whole act of what I would like to call "positioning ourselves in certain ways", could be one that might be more appreciated and not tied to sensations of "rejection", "isolation", and may be "guilt"...and whatever else might come to mind when thinking about the term "boundaries".

Thoughts around boundaries/preferences started occupying my mind more again recently after I graduated from my Master's pro gram. While I was anticipating that I would feel as if I had fallen into a deep hole after this intense program came to an end, I tried to prepare for the New, that was about to hit me...or was I about to hit it? If I hit the New, would it look different than if the New hit me? What do we do when one routine comes to an end and a new one has not been established yet? How do we navigate the New and how might it impact our identities?

For me, the New was certainly going to impact my identity as a mother, a wife, a daughter, a sister, and a friend...and my identity as ME, MYSELF...the SELF that I had disconnected from so long ago…when I moved to a foreign country, became a student in a foreign system, started interacting in a foreign language…in a foreign culture, became a friend to foreign people, became a girl friend and then a wife to a foreign man…then became a moth er, then took on my husband's last name, then became a mother again…and a student again…and a graduate again. Oh, how life's pathways shape our identities…how our decisions become our compass and navigate our next steps…some of which we want to take and some of which we have to take.

And what happens to our preferences along the way? How could we hold on to old, valuable preferences (the ones who make us who we are) as we create new ones? And what if some of those new preferences are desired yet come with sacrifices? Looking back at the last 10 years, I created new preferences and many of them came with sacrifices. One of the biggest sacrifices came with the decision to go back to school. This decision was filled with worry, hesitation, and SO MUCH DESIRE. I knew that I needed to do it, and was afraid about the changes this would bring to my routine as a mother. While I believe that we all (my entire family and myself) grew from this grad school experience, the biggest cost I paid was letting go of a connection to myself. While I learned so much about myself on the one hand throughout my program, I lost an everyday connection to myself. My preferences were shaped around my family's needs, school assignments, my traineeship requirements, and the side jobs I had along the way. I felt as if I was in a hamster wheel...running and running and running...and then all of the sudden, from one day to the next, the wheel stopped and although I knew I could jump off, it was surreal and when I did, there was the hole...

I've been sitting in the hole for a few weeks now and although it can be a little dark down here sometimes, the darkness is good...it is heavy sometimes, but good. The hole helps me feeling grounded. It helps me gather all the fringes of MYSELF that I had thrown out there to meet all the expectations...of myself and others...hold all the preferences I had created but which caused a distance to MYSELF. As I sit here in my hole, I am weaving...I am weaving the fringes into new preferences...Old ones and New ones come together...and they add to the tapestry of my life.

Transitions are heavy to carry AND they are beautiful intersections of the Old and the New...the "what is no longer and not yet either"...

Here is your space to write to your "Self":

_____

_____

_____

_____

_____

_____

_____

_____

_____

_____

_____

_____

_____

_____

_____

_____

_____

Facing Obstacles

Have you ever felt like things were happening in life that made you question when will it ever get easy? I'm sure you have, with obstacles come the greatest lessons. Lessons on how to tackle them when they revisit and how to possibly help others through similar situations. Documenting these obstacles and what you learned in a way starts to create a playbook for the next time they come at you. For me personally I like to document my obstacle to help me celebrate my wins in the end and as a mentioned use them as a playbook. This writer reflects on how them not giving up helped them push through. Check it out:

Dear Self Facing Obstacles,

All my life you thought failing was unacceptable when in actuality failure is acceptable. Failure have taught you multiple things. Most importantly it taught you perseverance. Perseverance is being persistence in doing something despite difficulty or delay in achieving   success. You have faced multiple obstacles chasing your dreams, but I beg you not to give up. Sometimes you have to re route your plan in order to achieve your dreams but most importantly you   have to understand to follow God's route. Romans 5:3-5 states that "we rejoice in our sufferings, knowing that suffering produces endurance, and endurance produces character, and character produces hope, and hope does not put us to shame, because God's love has been poured into our hearts through the Holy Spirit who has been given to us". Sometimes when you run into an obstacle chasing your dreams you freeze up, feel like the world is over and helpless. Whenever you run into an obstacle and feel like the world is over do these steps; let it out (scream, cry etc.), breath, pray about it then lastly create a plan while accepting that obstacle and failure. Failure made you re route when you didn't get into a good grad school making you feel like your life is over. It took you six months to get back to yourself. But did you ever stop and realize in those six months you were working your ass off. Stop stressing over your failure and appreciate it. It was because of that failure that pushed you into all that unexpected success.   Failure is an option and sometimes is the best thing that can ever happen to you. It may not seem like it in the moment but remember when your life reroutes it's okay because you can achieve your dreams by going many different routes. Your dreams remain the same, but the route you want to take may not.

Sincerely,

Self.

Here is your space to write to your "Self":

Affirm:

I am worthy

I am powerful

I am capable

I AM FULL OF POTENTIAL

Unsure "Self"

Being unsure of yourself can show up as imposter syndrome, low self esteem and can even just be from being let down in the past. It can be viewed in different ways and while I encourage you to explore what it means for you if you are experiencing it, I am also glad to have this letter of an example of ways it can show up. Check it out:

Dear Unsure Self,

I know it has not been easy. There have been in stance in your life that have caused you to take a pause at almost every turn. You have been let down, rejected, disappointed and shut out. Still you are standing and breathing. My Hope for you is this; that you look into the mirror and what you see is brilliance. Focus on all of the many times you have been knocked down and gotten back up. Think about where you are and how far you've come. think about the little brown girls who are looking to you to lead the way. Think about where you want to be, what you want to do and how well you want to do it. Trust that while uncertainty is to be expected, being unsure of yourself is not. Trust the process, trust the timing, and trust yourself. Like you tell your daughter, " You are strong, You are brace, you are smart, you are kind, you fight for what's right, you are beautiful and you are amazing!"

Con Carino,

Here is your space to write to your "Self":

Young Adult

We all know adulthood is the biggest scam, this letter does not need much of an intro, lets dive in.

Dear Young Adult Self,

When I entered adulthood, I had very high expectations of what my adult life would look like.

I thought I had done everything "right." I mean everything I grew up thinking was the right path into adulthood. I went to college and received a Bachelor's degree, then I furthered my education by receiving a Master's degree. Before graduating, I secured a job at the top tech company in the world.

My salary was generous (roughly 70k), I thought I was going to be rich. I'm a single woman with no kids, of course that will be enough, or so I thought. I did not take into account federal taxes, state taxes, social security, 401k contributions, insurance, etc. So at the start of my new career I made very reckless financial decisions.

I bought a brand new car and a very expensive mattress because in my mind "I deserved nothing but the best." That statement, was literally my motto for my financial decisions. I made all these reck less purchases before receiving my first paycheck.

My first paycheck came and it was $1400. My rent alone was $1550, my car note was $400. Not to mention I had 10k in credit card debt with super high interest rates. I mention all of this be cause my expectations did not match up with reality. When that happened, I fell into a deep depression.

I was prescribed antidepressants because I was emotionally debilitated from my financial woes and the disappointment I felt that adulthood did not welcome me with open arms. I stopped going out, I stopped eating, I just felt lost all around. I cried so much everyday after work because I was working a job with a salary I thought was good and still couldn't afford shit. My credit score was dropping, I really felt like I couldn't get a good grip on my finances.

How did I get out of this? I had to start by taking ownership. In the beginning I blamed anything and everyone. I was so frustrated that my parents and college did not prepare me for adulthood. I didn't understand personal finances at all and I definitely did not understand taxes.

I started looking at different resources like personal finance pod casts just to get an idea on how other people in their 20's were managing their finances. I also enrolled in a debt management pro gram to lower the interest rate on my credit cards so I could actually pay the cards down. I automated my savings because I didn't even know how to save with my paycheck or the benefit of having a savings account.

For a while it felt like I didn't see any improvements, but after 6 months I started to see my savings grow and my credit card debt was slowly coming down.

It was really hard transitioning from a college student to an adult because most of my life I only knew how to be a student, and college doesn't teach you how to be a financially responsible adult.

Feeling overwhelmed by life can sometimes lead to depression and anxiety, the best thing to do is to seek help whether it's from a sup port group, mentor, or professional therapist.

As of today, my savings account is where I want it to be, and I have paid off all of my credit card debt. These things take time and just remember staying consistent is the only way you'll see the progress you want.

Here is your space to write to your "Self":

Affirm:

I can find home within myself

NO ONE ELSE HOLDS THE KEY TO MY HAPPINESS.

Past Relationship

Relationships can take us on some twists and turns. It is important we take the time to reflect on past relationships to highlight what we did and did not like in the relationship in an effort to move forward.

Dear Past Relationship, Thank you for healing the disconnect.

Between the end of last year until recent trying to be open mind ed and have real ass open and honest conversations, reevaluating my decisions and just find peace within myself.

A while back you asked me did you change. I can tell you what I saw from my perspective but that doesn't necessarily mean it's true. Throughout the course of life we all change. And in all honesty maybe during that snapshot moment, I changed.

With a switch of a title everything changed my world. Yes I loved being around you. I had hopes and expectations for us. I had my frustrations with certain situations. And at one point in I just thought I was someone holding you down and I wasn't enough for you. I also gave up and stopped fully communicating what mattered the most to me. Although you didn't tell me, I knew you were going through a lot and I figured I'd be a burden if I tell you about my problems or our problems. I apologize for failing to communicate. I can't expect to solve an issue or even make sense of it until I open up to discuss it with you or the person at hand. Otherwise, it is all in my head and that is never the best place to be.

And although it hurt and felt abrupt because we never actually talked about it until that moment when you said I don't think we should do this. I thank you for that and thank you for trying. It gave me clarity. Time to evaluate my decisions and time to invest in filling my own cup.

We say we are in love. We say that they complete me. But do they really? Truthfully at one point in time I may have felt as though I was in love. Don't get me wrong I still love him and forever will. But during that process of "being in love," I lost me. I forgot the things that mattered to me the most and what made me happy. I was so wrapped up in the moment and concerned about pleasing you and everyone else that I forgot to take time and take care of me. Within this I've learned that yes, I am showing up for you but I need to make sure to show up for myself too.

Always be consciously aware of the current situation you're in and how it makes you feel. You have to feel comfortable enough to have those uncomfortable conversation and be open minded to hear the other persons side of view. Verbally express your feelings, holding it in doesn't make it go away. It may reveal itself in your actions or thoughts, and when it does it may not come out the way you intended it to. Think to yourself, "Is this relationship adding to my value, does it makes feel refreshed and happy or drained, stressed, and empty?" Evaluate yourself and the relationship, whether it be in friends, partners, or family members. And know when to take time out for yourself so that you too can be the best version of yourself emotionally, physically, and spiritually.

Here is your space to write to your "Self":

Heartbroken

It is important to be patient with ourselves to process and heal through heartbreak. It is also important to be trans parent and honest with yourself, check out this letter to gain some support and understanding on a possible way to support yourself in processing:

Dear heartbroken self,

When you lose the person you love most in this world, promise me that you'll breathe into the pain. Acknowledge it. Give it a name.

Don't turn to drugs, alcohol or the warmth of another to numb your senses and fill the gaping hole inside your soul. Don't isolate yourself from the people who love you most. Don't create a for tress around your heart so no person, place or thing can penetrate the darkness. Don't let this unfortunate event turn into a series of unfortunate events — transforming you into a shell of the wonderful human being you once were.

I know it hurts. I know that every time you look beside you, wishing that you could feel them once again, that your heart breaks into a million tiny pieces and blows away in the wind. I know that you when you wake up in the morning, for a few moments you're in bliss because you forgot that they're gone... and then reality sets in. What you wouldn't give to have another hour, another minute, an other second, to turn back time and relive the everyday moments that are now just memories you hold in your heart.

I'm not going to tell you that they are in a better place or that they're not suffering anymore. That's what people tell you, so you can feel better and move on. But I don't want you to move on because that means you'll forget.

Here are the facts. God blessed you with an angel that guided you through life and made you the person you are today. They taught you right from wrong, supported you, loved you unconditionally and believed in every single dream you had. Just because they're gone from this world does not mean that they don't live inside you. Matter cannot be created nor destroyed — so, they're still here, you just can see them. They're watching over you as you study for your exams, walk across the stage to get your diploma, fall in love with the human of your dreams and embark on your quest to change the world.

Through all the tears, gut-wrenching sobs and silent nights, re member that God has a plan and you are the light. Remember that your ancestors sacrificed for you to be able to experience life as you know it. Remember that just because your heart is broken and you feel like you can't take another loss, that you are right where you are meant to be and they will be with you always.

When bad things happen and we lose the people we love the most in this world, we must carry on in their memory. We must live fully and embrace the fleeting moments of happiness. Because when we look back, those fleeting moments are all we have.

So, pick yourself up, wash your face and put on your armor to fight for another day. Another day of love, light, and happiness.

Here is your space to write to your "Self":

Anxious

This letter is unique because we all cope with anxiety in different ways. In this letter the writer is writing out her experience and how she helps herself through her moments of anxiety; this letter can even be used when experiencing an anxiety attack. I encourage you to write one and maybe also write one on a small piece of paper that you can keep with you. Check it out:

Dear Anxious Self,

Stop. Breathe in, breathe out. It's going to be okay. You are not in danger -- this is your body's natural flight or fight response. How you feel is okay, and it will pass. Stop. Breathe in, breathe out. Once you understand your anxiety, it will be easier to control. Notice that you tend to assume the worst. Notice your internal dialogue and how mean you are to yourself. Notice the downward spiral that commences once you worry about that one thing, again.Stop. Breathe in, breathe out.

Try to rationalize how you feel. No, you're not running out of time. You're so young -- your whole life is still unwritten. Why not take it page by page? Stop. Breathe in, breathe out. Don't worry about what others think. It's okay to make mistakes -- you're only human. Remember that tomorrow is a new day, a clean slate, a fresh start.

Stop. Breathe in, breathe out.

All my love,

Here is your space to write to your "Self":

Self Conscious Self

Living in the age of social media has made it so hard for us as humans not be self conscious. Take some time to reflect on what it means to BE YOU, LOVE YOU and ADMIRE ALLTHAT YOUARE. Check out this letter below as the writer reflects on her experience and starts to rethink some things:

Dear Self-Conscious Self,

As you scroll down the endless black hole that is social media, all you can do is fixate on her body -- the perfect skin, poreless faced, smooth, tan legs. Oh, why can't you look like her?

Want to know the truth? That model doesn't even look like that picture. Our world is obsessed with altering our image: nip tuck here, plump there, snip here. All for a finished product: supposed, "perfection."

Guess what? You don't deserve that world. Why strive for so called, "perfection" when you're already your natural, beautiful self? You deserve self-love. To love those thick, strong thighs.

Treasure those natural curves that are smooth like honey. To rock your curly hair that shimmers in the golden sun.

No longer will you compare yourself to others. You are you, and that makes you, YOU-nique.

Your journey towards self-love starts now.

Love,

Me

Here is your space to write to your "Self":

Discouraged Self

What are some of the thoughts that come to your head when you feel discouraged? Probably things like " I should just give up" " why am I doing this anyway" … These exact thoughts are important to write out especially in a letter because when you ask why you are doing what you are doing you can take some to remind yourself of the why that you started with in the beginning.

Check out this letter below as the writer writes through a time of feeling discouraged.

Dear Discouraged Self,

In this present moment, it's hard and life has knocked you down. You've heard one too many "no's." Multiple doors have been slammed in your face. People have been removed from your life. Too many voices have been interjecting to tell you that your dreams are unachievable. Even you yourself are starting to believe that you are not good enough, that you are not smart enough, that you are not worthy of greatness.

It's time to snap back to reality. It's time to remember the BIGPICTURE. You were put on this Earth to impact positive change, to make a difference, to make our communities a better place for future generations. Your voice matters. Your opinions hold weight.

You as a human being, in all your faults and glory were meant to go through this experience.

Even though you have no money in your bank account and no food in your belly, YOU CANNOT GIVE UP. Not now. Not when you've overcome so many obstacles to become the human you are today.

You've come too far to throw the towel in. Your ancestors gave their lives to ensure that your generation and the generations to come, could have a better life.

You can't give up now. Not when future generations and dozens of little boys and little girls that you don't even know, are looking up to you.

It's your turn to write the history of your family. To create generational wealth. To change the trajectory of your family for generations to come.

So, I know it's hard. I know that the last thing you want to do is to get up and fight for another day but you have to. If you can't do it for you, do it for your parents, do it for your grandparents, do it for your ancestors.

Do it for the world because your purpose is to bring about change.

Keep your head up,

Discouraged self

Here is your space to write to your "Self":

Grieving Self

Grief is tough. Talk about an emotional rollercoaster; you never know when it is going to hit you. This is one of those subjects where there is no right thing to say but expressing yourself and letting it out is key.

Check out this writers experience with grief:

Dear Grief,

You visit again and again. Can I please be left alone today? I cover my grief with a smile and the idea that because I'm a therapist I have it all together? Definitely not, nights spent missing those who have made impact on my life and questioning why they will never be able to see the big moments of buying a house, having children and etc pains me. Oh to give my sweet aunt a hug and kiss again. To meet up at fancy restaurants and laugh all night. To complain about everyone who is annoying me only to hear her say "make sure you treasure people, they mean well." I think what hurts the most is knowing that I opened up so much to someone who I thought would always be there and now to look at pictures and to feel pain.

A pain that the pictures can't talk back. Nothing anyone says feels good but when your voice replays in my head I find my grounding. When I work hard or workout (lol) you appear. Grief, can you help me find peace in my heart? Even for a moment? Probably not. But I will remind myself of my precious aunts mottos she lived by, favorite scents and all of our adventures. I do them in honor of her. It's interesting how we experience grief with different people in different areas of life. I hope I'll be okay; I've got some faith in me.

Here is your space to write to your "Self":

Discovering Self

I am sure you can guess what this letter is all about. I want to remind you that self discovery can happen multiple times throughout your life. No matter where you are in the journey embrace it!

Discovering Self this is for you: I see you almost everyday...most days. But then the question "How did I get here" or "Why are you allowing this to continue" constantly cycles in your thoughts. You don't HAVE to be this way. I think growing up not being told how beautiful you were or being reminded that you are worthy, as much as you would have liked to have been told, has really taken a toll on you. Hearing the kids or people around you call you names for being dark skin or having "nappy" hair didn't help much either, huh? Then getting a little older & being told "You're pretty for a black/dark skin girl." I mean, that isn't much of a compliment. It's backhanded. You would think "Well why 'for a dark skin girl'?" I just want to feel and be 100% connected to being a black woman— to love me for me, and not have to feel insecure or sorry about it!

When you're insecure, it shows up everywhere, like, fuck. Stop following me! It shows up in places like your friendships, your career, but mainly in your love life. Ohhh, how it sucks that you've allowed past relationships with men who did not treat you the way you should have been treated to affect what you have now. What you have now is genuine, raw, vulnerability. He loves you & it's being shown everyday. Allow him to love you and teach him the little things that you'd like for him to do that he couldn't possibly know on his own because he isn't in your thoughts the way that you are. Nurture yourself even more so, so that the relationship can be even better than what it is. Remind yourself "You are beautiful, you are worthy, and he really does love you." You have this guard up, ready to fight when there's no need to here. It's safe. Remember, you're safe. Guess what, Insecure Self? You're getting evicted. There's no longer a home for you here! You have been on the court & doing the work. You are in therapy. You have let her close friends and loved ones know what she's battling so that they can better understand and hold her accountable! You even putting together an affirmation wall to affirm all of the things that she is and what she is manifesting for herself. The constant reminders sound like:

You are beautiful

You are worthy [to love and be loved fully, wholeheartedly]

You are bold

You are unique

You are capable of creating peace & living in it

You are fearless

You are resilient

You are a strong [black] woman

You are courageous

You are happy

You are independent

You are colorful

You are talented

You are wise

You are joyful

There will be a point where I won't be writing to "Insecure Self ". I'll be writing to "Confident Self ". I'm giving myself the love that I want & it's not that I wasn't loved. It was just different. I've been standing & owning my truth, no matter how embarrassing it may sound. It's where I am currently & I will not be stagnant. While I was shopping for home decor the other day, I came across an accent pillow that said, "Enjoy the ride," and I'm doing just that.

Here is your space to write to your "Self":

Chosen Self

We all want to feel accepted in some sense. We look to be accepted in childhood and that does not change in adulthood. But there is work to do to get there. If you feel you may be struggling with low self esteem this is for you. Check out a letter to chosen self to get an example here:

Dear Chosen Self,

All your life you have searched to be chosen and adored. From childhood to adulthood. In childhood you felt alone because your dad got married and began a family with your stepmom; you never felt that you fit in but you tried and because it didn't work you isolated yourself. You struggled with feeling like you were unwanted and searched to be showered with love from everywhere. You couldn't let your guard down out of fear that you would be hurt. You dated and never let them see the real you because you knew it wouldn't last. You were chosen to be a mom but didn't feel ready and still regret letting a beautiful opportunity pass you by. The one time you were chosen! In your relationship, you never feel chosen because you see that your boyfriend likes and follows women with body types you will never have. You look to him to validate you and assure you that you are chosen and yet he tells you that you can do that yourself. So again you don't feel chosen. You try to look within yourself to feel chosen and you do, but that does not mean you cannot be chosen by others. You want to feel special and loved by others unconditionally. You want it from friends, lovers and loved ones. Will they ever give it to you? Have you told them what it means to be chosen. To be chosen means that you have a special place in one's heart, they do not seek out others in comparison or in replacement of you. This is for both romantic relationships and friendships. It is highlighted that you are important and all that is needed. You are chosen. So where do we go from here? Do you build yourself up to choose yourself? The answer is unclear but you must keep searching. Do not give up for you will be chosen.

Here is your space to write to your "Self":

Discouraged Self

There is strength in recognizing when you are feeling discouraged. The strength is a bold statement that you have recognized where you are, the next step is doing what is needed for you to move forward. Check out a letter from someone having the experience of feeling discouraged below:

Dear discouraged self,

I noticed you come around when I least expect it, right when I'm feeling good about myself and/or life. You arrive uninvited with your self-doubt and confusion, taking up space that is not meant for you. Why do you come to steal my joy? Why do you come to tell me I'm not good enough? Why are you here interrupting my peace? Is it to throw me off my game? Is it to keep me at a place where I forget I have a crown to keep straight? It has worked before, but not this time. Discouragement shows up when there is an adjustment or change that I am resisting. understanding that change is inevitable and adjustments are consistently needed in all areas of life has allowed me to refuse you, discouragement at the door. Change can happen all at once, or little by little over time and I may not be ready for it, but what's true is that god is always ready and he will always allow the time necessary to make adjustments. I commit myself to not only thanking god for this time I've been given, but to use that time to process the changes around me, make adjustments accordingly, make an action plan, and then act on that plan. Now is the time to let go of any discouraging thoughts and push through these changes. If I begin to feel discouraged again, there's possibly an adjustment that needs to be made somewhere, it is not the end. Take a step back, process what is there, and make adjustments accordingly. After that, If I'm still feeling discouraged, I will write it out and pray it out. But I will process it and move on so I can get back to being Queen. Discouragement I thank you, for not naming you, I would not be able to overcome you. goodbye.

Here is your space to write to your "Self":

Now to tap into your Sense of Self, this is literally however you interpret it. While I did not expect this letter to tap into specially; I think it is something to think about. How do you think of and see yourself? How does this impact your journey? This letter dives right into it:

My sense of self will always be multidimensional. She is her. Her is me. I am this, that, and that too. Always. All ways. I am constantly growing and expanding in each moment. I am empty, yet I am full. Could I do more? Am I doing too much? Expansion remains on the horizon of my mind. See? as vast as the blue sea, only I can allow me to shrink. I have no objections to exploration; with risks and hopefulness, I've learned to own this. Own me. To greet this sense of self with trust, openness, and vulnerability; now you meet me authentically.

SENSES OF SELF

SENSES OF SELF

SENSES OF SELF

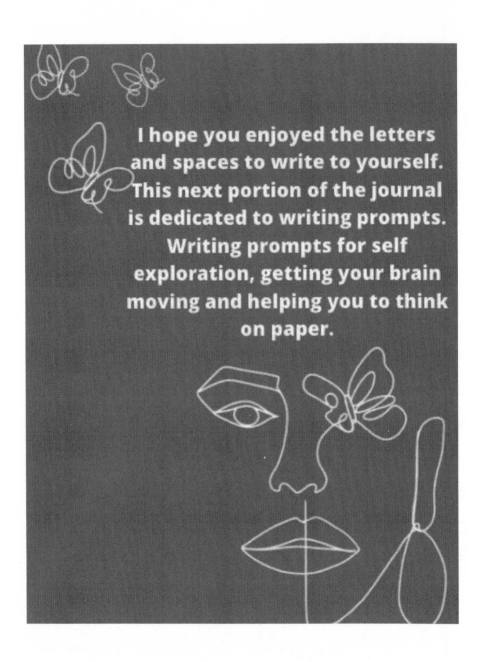

I hope you enjoyed the letters and spaces to write to yourself. This next portion of the journal is dedicated to writing prompts. Writing prompts for self exploration, getting your brain moving and helping you to think on paper.

Prompt: When I think of where I am currently and who I want to be what comes to mind is:

_____

_____

_____

_____

_____

_____

_____

_____

_____

_____

_____

_____

_____

_____

Think about what you wrote, what affirmation do you need to tell yourself in relation to your writing:

_____

_____

_____

_____

_____

_____

_____

_____

_____

_____

_____

_____

_____

_____

_____

Prompt: When I think of some things I have struggled to let go, what comes to mind is:

Letting things go is easier said than done. I challenge

you to think of ways you can push through the hurt

that is caused by what you are holding on to.

Next I invite you to give yourself grace.

Please be reminded that you are human and

sometimes letting go is tough.

Prompt: Who is someone you need to forgive? How will life be different once you do this?

We often times forget that forgiving others is more so for our benefit than for there's.

A way to affirm yourself in this forgiveness can be done by reminding yourself "I forgive for the lightness in my heart to appear" or whatever statement is best for you.

Try creating a statement here:

I forgive others to create space for

Prompt: We have all experienced grief. Think of some ways you want to/do honor those who you are or are currently grieving:

_____

_____

_____

_____

_____

_____

_____

_____

_____

_____

_____

_____

_____

Think about what you wrote; what affirmation do you need to tell yourself in relation to your writing:

_____

_____

_____

_____

_____

_____

_____

_____

_____

_____

_____

_____

_____

Prompt: How do I define happiness? How do I ensure that I have happiness in my life? (think only of how you do this and do not let material things make you feel you cannot be happy)

_____

_____

_____

_____

_____

_____

_____

_____

_____

_____

_____

_____

_____

_____

_____

Today I am:

Grateful

_____

Happy for

_____

I am thankful to have

_____

in my life.

Prompt: Recall a moment in your life where you felt most proud of yourself. Explain why you felt proud.

Think about what you wrote; what affirmation do you need to tell yourself in relation to your writing:

_____

_____

_____

_____

_____

_____

_____

_____

_____

_____

_____

_____

_____

_____

Prompt: What is your interpretation of love? Where did you learn this? What pieces of what you understand do you want to hold on to? What about let go of?

Prompt: Do I allow myself to be my whole self to others? What do I hold back? Why do I do this?

Prompt: How can I be more of my authentic self with others?

_____

_____

_____

_____

_____

_____

_____

_____

_____

_____

_____

_____

_____

_____

Today my:

Intentions are

_____

Hope for the day is

_____

Self care will be

_____

Thoughts:

Message from the author

Here is a message for you, remember that in moments of *anger* it is okay to feel your feelings. When you are feeling alone know that you are cared about. *Insecurities* come up, remind yourself that you are the (fill in words to empower yourself). In moments of *content* be sure to write it out so you don't forget the moment. On the journey of finding yourself remember to have patience with yourself. In your moments of *fear* remember fear is normal. *Disappointment* happens, take a moment for yourself during those times. Welcome in the forever *changes* of live and step out of your *comfort zone*. When you feel like *hiding* know that in those moments take some time to *pick yourself up*. Honor all the *boundaries* you set out in your life. In the face of *obstacles* know that you can overcome and silence your *unsure self* with positive self-talk. Dear *heartbreak*, you will feel whole again and when you feel *discouraged* bring back the reminder of patience with yourself. Remember the journey will have some confusion, discouraging moments, anxiety and other sense of self will be experienced.

The journey is worth traveling!

I hope you enjoyed, please note formatting is different on all letters to reflect that all are unique